Macdonald Daly was born in ~~Glasgow in 1963~~.
After graduating from the University of Glasgow
in 1984, he went to Balliol College, Oxford,
where he is working on a D.Phil. in English
Literature.

Alexander George hails from Manhattan. An
undergraduate at Columbia College, he received
his doctorate in philosophy from Harvard University in 1986 and is now Junior Research Fellow
in Philosophy at Wolfson College, Oxford.

MARGARET THATCHER IN HER OWN WORDS

COMPILED BY MACDONALD DALY AND ALEXANDER GEORGE

With an Introduction by
Sir Evan Covet

PENGUIN BOOKS

Penguin Books Ltd, Harmondsworth, Middlesex, England
Viking Penguin Inc., 40 West 23rd Street, New York, New York 10010, U.S.A.
Penguin Books Australia Ltd, Ringwood, Victoria, Australia
Penguin Books Canada Ltd, 2801 John Street, Markham, Ontario, Canada L3R 1B4
Penguin Books (N.Z.) Ltd, 182–190 Wairau Road, Auckland 10, New Zealand

First published 1987

Made and printed in Great Britain by
Richard Clay Ltd, Bungay, Suffolk
Set in 10 on 12pt. Monophoto Photina

To Agnes McAuley
and Sue Vice

ACKNOWLEDGEMENTS

We have received much help and tolerated much interference. Especially appreciated were those who turned a blind eye to – or better, even humoured – our more dubious ideas. Among these we would like to thank: the Five Vices; the JBs; Professor Gregory Clark; Stephen Blacklocks; Gordon 'the Black' Riddell; John F. Robins; Colin Troup; N. D. H.; Jo and the many Andrews, including Andrew Franklin, our editor at Penguin; and our families. Special thanks to Sir Evan Covet for his unbelievable co-operation and for taking time away from his many other duties to provide us with an Introduction. None of the above are responsible, of course, for any errors, other than having encouraged us in the first place.

M.D.
A.G.

INTRODUCTION
by Sir Evan Covet

Margaret Thatcher is the greatest leading lady of all time. At a stage in their history when the noble British people had abandoned their time-honoured values – those virtues of Christianity, enterprise, industry and many other guiding principles that they had so generously bequeathed to less endowed peoples – at such a nadir in our hitherto glorious history, Mrs Thatcher lifted us and set us right. We were like irresponsible children, always losing our way in pursuit of self-gratification, until she called us home.

And not a moment too soon. The Kremlin and its fifth column in this land had driven a red wedge into the body politic and threatened the very foundations of our democratic way of life. Rubbish-ridden streets, the dead denied burial, the sick and elderly refused care, our children crazed by punks and drugs, tradi-

9

tional family roles under fire. No one could or should forget. It was not a winter of discontent, it was a winter of disaster.

Our house was in disarray. It needed this woman's touch, this Great Housekeeper who gave our nation a good spring-cleaning. She flushed out the reds, shook down the trade unions, and scrubbed the metropolitan councils. Our Augean stables now cleared, she attended to their protection from the elements. Looking west, she found the ideal partner to secure the home from external attack. Strong and commanding, President Reagan has proved to be Mrs Thatcher's perfect leading man.

Traditional British qualities were resurrected. The nation could once again take pride in hard work, thrift, respect for authority, patriotism and the Church. Ever vigilant, Mrs Thatcher still maintains her guard. She has set her chin squarely against those who encourage idleness, extravagance, lawlessness and unnatural acts: the whining unemployed, self-seeking immigrants, murderous hooligans and godless perverts.

No longer can people holiday at the State's expense

or reap a workless wage. No longer is British culture threatened with dilution. No longer is the policeman fettered and the criminal free. No longer need rate-payers subsidize the follies of lifestyles alien to those of our people.

These have not been easy victories. Mrs Thatcher has had to contend not only with the crowing of hardened extremists, but with the bleating of the faint-hearted and lily-livered too. An account of all this and more can now be found in this choice selection from our leader's words, a compilation uncoloured by partisan commentary or editing, and free from the usual political pettifoggery which so hinders an objective appreciation of these great achievements.

Readers of this collection, the work of two young Oxford men, will find much humour, inspiration and insight in the words of this singular and extraordinary lady. It is especially appropriate that the very Oxford spires which spawned and later spurned her* should now spread her wisdom far and wide.

* On Oxford's disgraceful denial of an honorary degree to Mrs Thatcher, see my letter to *The Times*, 6 January 1985.

Economics are the method; the object is to change the soul.

The Sunday Times, 3/5/81

The mission of this government is much more than the promotion of economic progress. It is to renew the spirit and solidarity of the nation.

Speech in Cambridge, 6/7/79

I call the Conservative Party now to a crusade. Not of the Conservative Party. I appeal to all those men and women of good will who do not want a Marxist future for themselves or their children or their children's children.

For this is not just a fight about national solvency. It is a fight about the very foundations of the social order. It is a crusade not merely to put a temporary block on socialism but to stop its onward march once and for all.

The Times, 9/10/76

In other words, I want to get totally rid of class distinction. As someone put it in one of the papers this morning: Marks and Spencer have triumphed over Karl Marx and Engels.

The Times, 6/5/85

I want a capital-earning democracy. Every man and woman a capitalist. Housing is the start. If you're a man or woman of property, you've got something. So every man a capitalist, and every man a man of property.

Observer, 8/5/83

I came to office with one deliberate intent; to change Britain from a dependent to a self-reliant society — from a give-it-to-me to a do-it-yourself nation; to a get-up-and-go, instead of a sit-back-and-wait-for-it Britain.

The Times, 9/2/84

What stands in our way? The prospects of another winter of discontent? I suppose it might, but I prefer to believe that certain lessons have been learnt from experience, that we are coming slowly, painfully to an autumn of understanding. I hope it will be followed by a winter of common sense.

If it is not, we shall not be diverted from our course. To those waiting with bated breath for that favourite media catch-phrase, the U-turn, I have only one thing to say: You turn if you want; the lady's not for turning.

Speech to the Conservative Party Conference, 10/10/80

I had the most marvellous upbringing; it stayed with me the rest of my life. It was, I always thought, a very tough upbringing. I was taught from my early years at school, taught by my father, to make up my own mind about my views, to say, 'This is what I believe in, this is what I am going to do.' Then you perhaps find that maybe the crowd comes with you. But never go with the crowd for the sake of going with the crowd – never, never, never. My goodness, it was hard as a young person; it was hard, but it was right.

Sunday Telegraph, 14/2/82

I shall be a radical Prime Minister for my second term of office because I am radically right.

Director, September 1983

I am painted as the greatest little dictator, which is ridiculous – you always take some consultations.

The Times, 8/6/83

———◀◆◆▶———

[On other EEC Heads of State.] There are nine of them being tiresome, and only one of me. I can cope with the nine of them, so they ought to be able to stand one of me. They could end the tiresomeness and stubbornness by giving me what I want.

The Times, 10/4/84

[Asked what her view would be if sanctions against South Africa were the only way to keep the Commonwealth together.] But if I were the odd one out and I were right, that would not matter, would it?

The Times, 14/6/86

Deep in their instincts, they [the majority of people] find what I am saying and doing right, and I know it is, because that is the way I was brought up. I'm eternally grateful for the way I was brought up in a small town. We knew everyone, we knew what people felt. I sort of regard myself as a very normal, ordinary person with all the right, instinctive antennae.

The Sunday Times, 3/8/80

I love argument, I love debate. I don't expect anyone just to sit there and agree with me, that's not their job.

The Times, 5/5/80

I go for agreement, agreement for the things I want to do.

The Times, 10/4/84

When I was young I was taught at home this little doggerel:

> It's easy to be a starter,
>   But are you a sticker too?
> It's easy enough to begin a job,
>   It's harder to see it through.

A determination to stick with the task of making Britain a more hospitable climate for freedom and enterprise would be, I feel, a good resolution for 1984 – and the rest of the decade.

Reader's Digest, January 1984

I believe in the acceptance of personal responsibility, freedom of choice, and the British Empire, which took freedom and the rule of law to countries which would never have known it otherwise.

The Times, 18/2/83

Our first duty to liberty is to keep our own. But it is also our duty – as Europeans – to keep alive in the Eastern as well as the Western half of our continent those ideas of human dignity which Europe gave to the world.

Let us therefore resolve to keep the lamps of freedom burning bright so that all who look to the West from the shadows of the East need not doubt that we remain true to those human and spiritual values that lie at the heart of European civilization.

The Times, 25/6/77

I am convinced that there is little force left in the Marxist stimulus to revolution. Its impetus is petering out as the practical failures of the doctrine become more obvious ... What is left is a technique of subversion and a collection of catch-phrases.

The former is still dangerous. Like terrorism, it is a menace that needs to be fought whenever it occurs.

The Times, 19/12/79

I believe our way of life is infinitely superior for every human being than any which the Communist creed can offer.

The Times, 5/5/80

That is what capitalism is: a system that brings wealth to the many, not just to the few.

Speech to Joint Meeting of US Congress, 20/2/85

You know the critical thing with the Communist countries is Communism, which by definition consists of control by the government.

The Times, 31/1/87

Life in a free society . . . is heaven on earth to life in a socialist society such as Russia.

House of Commons, 5/6/86

We must not fall into the trap of projecting our own morality onto the Soviet leaders. They do not share our aspirations, they are not constrained by our ethics, they always consider themselves exempt from the rules that bind other states.

The Times, 30/9/83

Is there conscience in the Kremlin? Do they ever ask themselves what is the purpose of life? What is it all for? ... No. Their creed is barren of conscience, immune to the promptings of good and evil.

The Times, 30/9/83

The Russians are bent on world domination.

The Times, 20/1/76

While the Soviet Union has imposed its rule on its neighbours and drawn an iron curtain between east and west, we in Great Britain have given freedom and independence to more than forty-eight countries whose populations now number more than a thousand million – a quarter of the world's total.

The Times, 30/9/83

The Russians put guns before butter. We put just about everything before guns.

The Times, 20/1/76

To many of us it seems there is precious little difference between the policies of the Communist Party and the policies of the Labour Party.

The Times, 12/12/80

By 'they' I mean that somewhat strange alliance between the comrades of the Russian Defence Ministry and our Defence Ministry.

The Times, 2/2/76

And what a prize we have to fight for: no less than the chance to banish from our land the dark divisive clouds of Marxist socialism.

Speech to the Scottish Conservative Conference, 13/5/83

The cuts are not divisive. Too much state spending is divisive. It divides the honest saver from the profligate spender. It favours those who live for the day rather than those who provide for the morrow.

The Times, 22/5/80

I am much nearer to creating one nation than Labour will ever be. Socialism is two nations. The privileged rulers, and everyone else. And it always gets to that. What I am desperately trying to do is create one nation with everyone being a man of property, or having the opportunity to be a man of property.

The Sunday Times, 27/2/83

Liberty and property are intricately bound up in our history; and a country that has no property rights has no human rights ... You cannot have freedom without capital and private property in the hands of the people.

Reader's Digest, January 1984

My main reason for hope lies in the character of the British people. We've always shown great industrial ability and enterprise. We've always been outward-looking. From Elizabethan times this country has thrived because the people have gone overseas seeking trade; so I believe we have a world perspective.

Reader's Digest, **January 1984**

———◆◆◆▶———

[On the beer mat which showed her as a cross between a vulture and a pecking hen and the china toilet-roll-holder shaped like her head.] I didn't like that. People don't do that sort of thing, it's not British.

Daily Express, 13/8/80

[On criticism of Kenny Everett's remark about bombing the Russians.] I really just begin to wonder what has happened to the British sense of humour.

The Times, 8/6/83

We are a British nation with British characteristics. Every country can take some small minorities and in many ways they add to the richness and variety of this country.

The moment the minority threatens to become a big one, people get frightened.

World in Action, 30/1/78

Citizenship should be based on those who have a close and real relationship with this country and its inhabitants.

The Times, 4/11/76

If we went on as we are then by the end of the century there would be four million people of the New Commonwealth and Pakistan here.

Now, that is an awful lot and I think it means that people are really rather afraid that this country might be rather swamped by people of a different culture and you know, that the British character has done so much for democracy, for law, and done so much throughout the world that if there were any fear that it might be swamped, people are going to react and be rather hostile to those coming in. So, if you want good race relations you have got to allay people's fears on numbers.

World in Action, 30/1/78

[To US tourists wondering whether they should travel to Britain after the US attack on Libya.] Please come. Please change your mind. Not only does it help our standard of living, our economy, but we miss you. We like seeing you. We love your friendliness. We love your warmth. We love your generosity and we are missing it on our streets . . . Life is normal. Come. We miss you.

Interview on US television; quoted in *The Times* 24/5/86

———◄◆◆►———

This party is pro-American.

The Times, 13/10/84

[On the US administration.] We see so many things in the same way and you can speak of a real meeting of minds. I feel no inhibitions about describing the relationship as very, very special.

Financial Times, 23/2/85

[On Ronald Reagan.] The election of a man committed to the cause of freedom and the renewal of America's strength has given encouragment to all those who love liberty.

Speech to the United Nations, 28/2/81

I support very much the approaches that the President is taking. As you know, I am his greatest fan.

The Times, 18/2/85

[On Ronald Reagan.] The West could have no better or braver champion.

Speech to the Conservative Party Conference, 11/10/85

It is with friends you can talk frankly. Never with rancour. Always with friendship. Always with understanding. That is the way it is between Britain and the United States. And that is the way it will always be.

Daily Telegraph, 10/12/83

The United States is contributing massively to the defence of Europe and we should be very grateful.

Hansard, **27/10/83**

We are very fortunate to have someone else's weapons stationed on our soil, to fight those targeted on us.

Time, **16/2/81**

I do not understand the unilateralists. If they hated nuclear weapons as much as I do they would want them down in the world as a whole. I am the true disarmer. I keep peace and freedom and justice with it.

The Times, 17/1/83

Both the President and Mr Gorbachev have said that they want to see a world without nuclear weapons. I cannot see a world without nuclear weapons. Let me be practical about it. The knowledge is there to make them. So do not go too hard for that pie in the sky because, while everyone would like to see it, I do not believe it is going to come about.

The Times, 28/3/86

It is absolutely right that President Reagan considers SDI, and thank goodness people considered nuclear research before the last world war.

House of Commons, 17/2/87

For several years after the war the United States had a monopoly of nuclear weapons, but was a threat to no one. Democracies are naturally peace-loving ... the use of force or the threat of force are no part of our philosophy. The radical proposals for disarmament on the table now come from the West. It is the response from Moscow which is deficient ... No amount of propaganda, of spurious half-truths can disguise the determination of the Soviet Union to maintain or gain numerical advantage in weaponry, men and materials. No amount of facile argument can conceal the fact that Soviet flexibility to date has been designed to beguile public opinion, not to make progress.

The Times, 30/9/83

We are the true peace movement.

The Times, 29/4/83

[Asked whether Polaris would be launched in the event of a Soviet conventional attack in Europe.] Of course, I would actually fire it.

Morning Star, 1/6/83

A bully has no respect for a weakling and the way to stop a bully is not to be weak. The way to stop a bully from ever being a bully is to say 'I'm as strong as you. Anything you do to me, I can do to you.' We are going for nuclear and conventional disarmament but we're going about it in the right way.

World This Weekend, 10/1/82

Me? A Cold Warrior? Well, yes – if that is how *they* wish to interpret my defence of values and freedoms fundamental to our way of life.

Speech to Finchley Constituents, 31/1/76

I'm not hard – I'm frightfully soft. But I will not be hounded. I will not be driven anywhere against my will.

Daily Mail, 8/2/72

There are times when I get home at night and everything has got on top of me when I shed a few tears, silently, alone . . . Anyone who does not [believe wholeheartedly in love] must be terribly unhappy . . . I often unwind by ironing or turning out the airing cupboard, which personally I find very relaxing.

Women's World, 21/9/78

Oh, I have got lots, lots of human weaknesses, who hasn't?

The Times, 8/6/83

I stand before you tonight in my chiffon evening gown, my face softly made up, my fair hair gently waved . . . The Iron Lady of the Western World?

Speech to Finchley Constituents, 31/1/76

[On the idea that she is an 'Iron Lady'.] Oh yes, I think it is a compliment. You have to have a touch of steel. You do need to be pretty firm in the defence of your country's interests.

Talk to under-twelves at Grantham High School for Girls, 6/6/80

We have done quite a lot fundamental with steel. Seventy thousand redundancies. All right, it has cost us a bit.

The Sunday Times, 3/5/81

It is ironic that we should be accused of wanting unemployment to solve our economic problems by the very government which has produced record postwar unemployment, and is expecting more.

Speech to the Conservative Party Conference, 10/10/75

Unemployment may be [long pause] an unpalatable consequence of fighting inflation.

The Sunday Times, 3/8/80

We Conservatives hate unemployment. We hate the idea of men and women not being able to use their abilities. We deplore the waste of national resources and the deep affront to people's dignity by being out of work through no fault of their own.

Speech to the Conservative Party Conference, 10/10/75

I think it's terrible if a person who wants to work cannot find a job. You have no self-respect, you haven't got the respect of your family, if somehow you cannot earn yourself a living and them a living too.

Sometimes I have heard it said that the Conservatives have been associated with unemployment. That is absolutely wrong. We would have been drummed out of office if we'd had this level of unemployment.

Party Political Broadcast, 4/5/77

Britain is one of the few countries which is creating jobs.

House of Commons, 8/5/85

The number of people in work has increased by 700,000 since October 1983 ... Yes, many of the jobs have been part-time, and what is wrong with that?

House of Commons, 30/1/86

I couldn't live without work. That's what makes me so sympathetic to these people who are unemployed. I don't know how they live without working.

News of the World, 4/5/80

We all care about unemployment ... I understand what it must be like for a man to search for a job day after day and too often month after month and not to find one.

I understand what it must be like not only for him, but for his family as well. Pride, dignity and self-respect go with a job ... But caring is not enough. You've got to do something about it.

Speech in Cardiff, 23/5/83

[On factory closures.] Every time, I think, gosh, what would I have done if my husband had come home and said we've got notice and there just don't seem to be any places to go.

The Sunday Times, 3/8/80

[On the role of Denis Thatcher.] Yes, I discuss a number of political things with him. He's absolutely marvellous on industry. We discuss the nationalized industries. He's great at looking through the balance sheets. I can say to him: 'Look, is this firm in difficulties or isn't it? Tell me. Look at the figures. Do you think they'll need to borrow, and how much?' I really can draw on his experience ... And then on broad issues he'll sometimes say: 'Look, you've gone too far this time. Don't get too intense about this problem.'

Daily Mail, 3/5/80

I do not have to worry about money . . . it is expensive to be in politics, one has to be well-groomed, and one has to entertain.

Guardian, 23/3/62

No one would have remembered the Good Samaritan if he'd only had good intentions. He had money as well.

Weekend World, 6/1/80

Where do new jobs come from? Who in pre-war days would have said there would be such a big nursery-garden industry? But you go and buy a rose in a pot and put it in your garden. So more leisure can also create jobs. People take package holidays. They pursue new hobbies. They put a great deal into having very much more nicely furnished houses, and do-it-yourself, and lovely gardens.

Director, September 1983

We must also expect that a lot more of our jobs will come from the service industries – from the McDonalds and the Wimpys, which employ a lot of people, from the kind of Disney Land they are starting in Corby. There is a great industry in other people's pleasures.

Director, September 1983

Young people ought not to be idle. It is very bad for them. It starts them off wrong ... They should not have the option of being unemployed.

The Times, 18/12/84

Pennies do not come from heaven. They have to be earned here on earth.

Sunday Telegraph, 14/2/82

[On a visit to the Commons of jobless youngsters.] I will put it to them that the economy is expanding, that investment is at an all-time record, the standard of living is at an all-time high and that there are great expansions in the Youth Training Scheme from which they will benefit.

The Times, 27/3/85

Sometimes the wages of young people are much too high in relation to the wages of adults, and employers just can't afford to take them on, although they would like to.

Director, September 1983

◄◆◆►

It is not social conditions that generate violence. Yes, unemployment breeds frustration, but it is an insult to the unemployed to suggest that a man who does not have a job is likely to break the law.

Speech to the Conservative Party Conference, 11/10/85

In their muddled but different ways the vandals on the picket lines and the muggers in our streets have got the same confused message: 'We want our demands met, or else,' and 'Get out of our way, give us your handbag, or else.'

The Times, 20/4/79

I don't believe people who go on strike in this country have legitimate cause.

Financial Times, 23/6/82

It is an appalling example to children that teachers should go on strike. Children think that all they have to do is the same to get their own way.

The Times, 22/6/84

A new attitude is prevailing as many employees are learning that democracy means the right to say no to your trade union as well as to your other boss.

The Times, 21/7/80

The Conservative Party is not hostile to Trade Unions, but believes in a strong and responsible Trade Union movement: strong to protect and represent interests of people at work; responsible in the way it uses its power.

The Times, 1/3/76

In my view and the view of many, many people, it would be a jolly sight better if the unions concentrated on representing the interests of their members at work and their leaders did not get involved in politics.

The Times, **26/4/79**

It is all very well talking about jobs but if they go on strike when they have got jolly good jobs, and jolly good pay, they are destroying jobs.

Director, **September 1983**

Whenever I go overseas they say: 'Stop strikes and we will buy your products,' and that I can't stop. People must understand that if they go on strike and they do themselves out of a job, that's their fault and the unemployment and the reputation Britain gets because of it is their fault; that is their responsibility.

The Times, 31/3/83

I don't like the idea of a trade unionist going to prison because it would be so very easy for him to say, look I went to prison for my beliefs, and I would have some sympathy for that.

Panorama, 25/2/80

[On the miners' strike.] The nation faces what is probably the most testing crisis of our time – the battle between the extremists and the rest. We are fighting as we have always fought, for the weak as well as the strong. We are fighting for just and good causes ... This government will not weaken, this nation will meet that challenge. Democracy will prevail.

The Times, 13/10/84

The facts are well known. This government has given a better deal to the mining industry than any previous government.

The Times, 20/6/84

Scabs, their former workmates call them. Scabs? They are lions. What a tragedy when a striking miner attacks his workmate. Not only are they members of the same union. But the working miner is saving both their futures.

The Times, 13/10/84

[On police conduct during the miners' strike.] I find it totally and utterly false to cast a slur on the police for the superb way they have handled this dispute.

The Times, 10/4/84

Enemy? The overwhelming majority of the British people regard the police as friends.

The Times, 12/10/85

[On the National Union of Mineworkers.] They have brought back the soup kitchen to Britain.

The Times, 29/10/84

The miners' strike objective was to stop the supply of power to industry so that it could bring industry and people to a dead stop, so that they would not have had jobs or a future, and to stop the supply of fuel to houses so they would have stopped it to the housewife and old people. They are the people who talk about compassion.

The Times, 18/2/85

I probably care more about the future of the coal industry than many Labour MPs.

The Times, 25/11/84

Surely, caring is what you do, not just what you say. And those who talk most are not always those who do most. We need no lessons in care from other parties. We want to solve our nation's problems not exploit them or disguise them. We are in politics because we care.

Speech to the Scottish Conservative Conference, 16/5/86

In about twenty-five years' time there will be quite a lot of people, who will be inheriting something, because for the first time we will have a whole generation of people who own their own homes and will be leaving them, so that they topple like a cascade down the line of the family, leaving to others not only their houses but some of their shares, some of their building-society investments, some of their national-savings certificates – only on a bigger scale than ever before.

The overwhelming majority of people, who could never look forward to that before, will be able to say: 'Look, they have got something to inherit. They have got the basis to start on!' That is tremendous. That is popular capitalism.

The Times, 28/3/86

It doesn't matter where you are, where you come from. If you can make a contribution to our society and if you can build up a future for yourself, if you can, jolly good luck to you. I want the successful people here. That is the sort of economy I am building; not an onerous society, but a go-getter society.

The Times, 10/4/84

Without the strong, who would provide for the weak?
When you hold back the successful you penalize those
who need help.

Speech to the Conservative Party Conference, 13/10/78

The Conservative Party does not believe in inequity.

The Times, **25/5/85**

[The Thatcher experiment] means more inequality but it means you drag up the poor people because there are more resources to do so.

The Times, 7/1/80

[Recalling her attendance at the 1946 Conservative Party Conference.] The platform seemed a long way away and I had no thought of joining the lofty and distinguished people sitting up there. But our party is the party of equality and opportunity – as you can see.

Speech to the Conservative Party Conference, 10/10/75

[On the Conservative Party.] The leading democratic party of the world.

The Times, 27/11/84

We Conservatives do not accept that because some people have no choice, no one should have it.

Speech to the Conservative Party Conference, 10/10/75

Let our children grow tall and some taller than others
if they have it in them to do so.

US Tour, September 1975

The way to recovery is through profits.

Speech to the Conservative Party Conference, 10/10/75

What I think people are saying to the government is this: 'You understood what worried us a few years ago. And you had the guts to do something about it. Do you understand what is worrying us today? And if you do, will you show the same guts and sort that out too?'

There is only one answer to that: 'Yes, yes and yes again.'

Speech to Scottish Conservative Conference, 16/5/86

———◄◆◆►———

Self-questioning is essential to the health of any society but we have perhaps carried it too far; and carried to extremes it causes paralysis. The time has come when the West – above all Europe and the United States – must begin to substitute action for introspection.

The Times, 19/12/79

I don't believe this country wants weak government. I don't believe they want a government to be so flexible that it becomes invertebrate. I think they want a government with a bit of spine. You don't want a government of flexi-toys.

Sun, 9/7/85

Which is better, the nurse who smothers the patient with sympathy and coddling, or the one who says: 'Now, come on, shake out of it. I know you have had an operation yesterday. It is time you put your feet on the ground and took a few steps. That's right, dear, that's right . . .'

Which is the one most likely to get results? The one who says 'Come on, you can do it.' That's me.

The Times, 1/12/80

I do take some consolation that there is only one small vowel sound between 'ruin' and 'run'. The small vowel sound is 'I'.

Speech to the New York Pilgrims Society, 17/9/75

◄◆◆►

It's like a patient, there's a time when you are still suffering from the disease and you take the medicine, and there is a time when you are suffering from both the disease and the medicine. That doesn't mean you stop the medicine, you know you have to take the medicine if you are to be cured of the disease ... The immediate effect of that, I am afraid, is increased interest rates, just as sometimes the immediate effect of an antibiotic can be rather damaging to your digestive system.

The Times, 5/5/80

After almost any major operation you feel worse before you convalesce. But you do not refuse the operation when you know that, without it, you will not survive ... We did not promise you 'instant sunshine'.

The Times, 13/3/80

Our whole philosophy is built on respect for the traditional moral values which are the cornerstones of a free society. All our policies are designed to encourage personal responsibility, personal initiative, self-respect and respect for others and their property.

Speech to Scottish Conservative Conference, 13/5/83

[On her upbringing.] You were taught to work jolly hard, you were taught to improve yourself, you were taught self-reliance, you were taught to live within your income, you were taught that cleanliness was next to godliness, you were taught self-respect, you were taught always to give a hand to your neighbour, you were taught tremendous pride in your country, you were taught to be a good member of your community.

The Times, 16/4/83

We had a very strict upbringing. We were never allowed to go to a cinema on a Sunday and were forbidden to play any games such as snakes and ladders. Although there were playing cards in the house, we were certainly never permitted to use them on that day. Of course my grandmother lived with us until she died, when I was ten years old, and she was very, very Victorian and very, very strict.

Patricia Murray, *Margaret Thatcher: A Profile*, 1980

Our grandparents and parents brought us up without trendy theories and they didn't make such a bad job of it.

Daily Mirror, 25/7/78

Parents have been told by self-appointed experts that their duties to each other should be balanced by more emphasis on self-fulfilment. In other words, we have seen the birth of the permissive society. Has that benefitted women? Far from it . . . We know that for our society as a whole and especially for the children, much depends on the family unit remaining secure and respected.

1952; quoted in *Cosmopolitan*, May 1983

There would be no difference if the government were run by women. A Cabinet of women would have to consider men voters just as much as the Cabinet considers women voters.

Guardian, 23/3/62

Of course it's very hard work being a housewife, apart from all the daily chores, there's the laundry, the shopping, the breakfast to get, the midday meal, tea and supper. However, in a way you have more of your life under your control – all right, you've got to get meals ready at certain times but you can decide what you're going to do next, what you're going to have to eat, how you arrange your room and who you're going to invite home.

Patricia Murray, *Margaret Thatcher: A Profile*, 1980

Many of the qualities which we women display quite naturally in our jobs here [in Parliament] are just those very same qualities that a woman who is running a home has – she has to be a good manager.

Central Lobby, 26/6/86

I hope we shall see more and more women combining marriage and a career. Prejudice against this dual role is not confined to men. Far too often, I regret, it comes from our own sex . . .

It is possible to carry on working, taking a short leave of absence when families arrive, and returning later. The idea that the family suffers is, I believe, quite mistaken. To carry on with a career stimulates the mind, provides a refreshing contact with the world outside – and so means that a wife can be a much better companion at home.

1952; quoted in *Cosmopolitan*, May 1983

I would think it impossible for a mother with young children to be an MP if she lives way out of London. She wouldn't see them for two or three days and she'd feel that she was missing so much.

Patricia Murray, *Margaret Thatcher: A Profile*, 1980

[On male Heads of State.] They don't patronize me for being a woman – NOBODY puts me down.

Daily Express, 13/8/80

[On François Mitterand.] He likes women, you know.

Ed. Hugo Young and Anne Sloman,
The Thatcher Phenomenon, 1981

The battle for women's rights has been largely won.

Guardian, 27/7/82

I feel terribly guilty I am not wearing blue, but I am going to the television studios and the background is bright turquoise – so I have to wear brown. We girls must think about these things.

The Times, 2/4/79

[On Party colour.] I adore *red*, but of course I can only wear it at home or on holiday. People really comment on it, you know.

Daily Telegraph, 5/10/64

[On being a public figure.] I once tried to go out in a headsquare and red glasses. But within ten minutes somebody had said 'Oh, hello, Mrs Thatcher.'

Talk to under-twelves at Grantham High School for Girls, 6/6/80

[On sunbathing.] I turn red and peel – I've never managed brown legs in my life.

Daily Express, 13/8/80

My job is to stop Britain from going red.

Speech to the Institute of Public Relations, 2/11/77

Step by step we are rolling back the frontiers of socialism and returning power to the people.

Speech to the Conservative Party Conference, 11/10/85

State socialism is totally alien to the British character.

The Times, 8/6/83

Today, instead of the voice of compassion, the croak of the Quango is heard in the land. There may not be enough jobs for the workers, but there are certainly plenty of jobs for the boys. Many in the Labour Party wonder what has happened to it. Socialism has gone sour. Today, Labour seems to stand too often for expedience, for greed, for privilege, for policies that set one half of society against the other. There are many other reasons for this. One stems from the least attractive of emotions, envy. The spirit of envy is aimed not only at those privileged by birth and inherited wealth, like Mr Wedgewood Benn. It is also directed against those who have got on by ability and effort. It is seen in Labour's bias against men and women who seek to better themselves and their families. Ordinary people – small businessmen, the self-employed – are not to be allowed to rise on their own. They must rise collectively or not at all.

Speech to the Conservative Party Conference, 13/10/78

Socialists have always seemed to me to assume that other people were creating a world for them to distribute.

Director, September 1983

Marxists get up early in the morning to further their cause. We must get up even earlier to defend our freedom. We must not allow ourselves the luxury of disunity.

Daily Mail, 13/5/78

[On public reaction to economic improvements under Labour.] They were so relieved they had not been submerged that they forgot they had to face forty years in the wilderness.

Speech to the Institute of Public Relations, 2/11/77

I sometimes think the Labour Party is like a pub where the mild is running out. If someone doesn't do something soon, all that's left will be bitter. And all that's bitter will be Left.

Speech to the Conservative Party Conference, 10/10/75

What the Labour Party of today wants is: housing municipalized; industry re-nationalized; the police service politicized; the judiciary radicalized; union membership dynamized; and, above all and most serious of all, our defence neutralized. Never. Never in Britain.

Speech to the Conservative Party Conference, 10/10/86

A Labour Britain would be a neutralist Britain. It would be the greatest gain for the Soviet Union in forty years. And they would have got it without firing a shot.

Speech to the Conservative Party Conference, 10/10/86

◄◆◆►

It is fashionable for some commentators to speak of the two superpowers, the United States and the Soviet Union, as though they were somehow of equal significance . . . that is a travesty of the truth . . . we do not aim at world domination, at hegemony in any part of the world.

Speech to Joint Meeting of US Congress, 20/2/85

The Soviet Union knows full well that I would be very careful not to get out of step with them [the Americans]. They are our greatest allies, the lynchpin of freedom and N A T O, and we have to stand together.

The Times, 22/12/84

As the United States and Britain are allies, we would always have had to accept any advice that the United States gave us. Indeed, it follows that we would not be free to accept or reject the advice of the United States.

Hansard, 27/10/83

————◄◆◆►————

The best basis of foreign policy is what is in the British interests.

House of Commons, 22/4/86

I believe that there is no country other than Libya where there is a government that has inspired such a remorseless campaign of terrorist attacks and where we have specific evidence of their complicity in these attacks.

Under the circumstances I believe that the United States was absolutely right and within its right to exercise its right to self-defence.

House of Commons, 15/4/86

The first duty of government is to uphold the law. If it tries to bob and weave and duck around that duty when it is inconvenient, if government does that, then so will the governed, and then nothing is safe – not home, not liberty, not life itself.

Speech to the Conservative Party Conference, 10/10/75

[On Grenada.] [The Americans] looked at it, as I said at the time, from a different aspect. I see no point in going back over it again. Most of the Americans are out. That's a fantastic contrast to the Soviet Union in Afghanistan.

The Times, 1/6/84

In Central America we keep troops stationed in Belize at that government's request. That is our contribution to sustaining democracy in a part of the world so vital to the United States.

Speech to Joint Meeting of US Congress, 20/2/85

We have previously made it very clear to the United States government that we are against mining the ports in Nicaragua because, of course, it is very dangerous to international traffic on the high seas.

Hansard, 10/4/84

The United States has no socialist party, and no socialist party has been in power. That is the reason why it has always been the country of last resort for every currency.

The Times, 1/6/84

In the United States, you have two parties based on free enterprise, freedom, and justice. Here the two main parties have two fundamentally different philosophies.

Director, September 1983

Q. The true opposition to you would be what?

A. Well, a different way of achieving the same objective.

Q. Within the same framework of free enterprise?

A. Yes, yes.

Q. More like Democrats and Republicans?

A. Yes, more like Democrats and Republicans

Director, September 1983

[On Labour and Conservative alternatives.] The choice between a society that is coerced and a society that is free under a rule of law.

The Times, 17/5/83

We are witnessing a deliberate attack on our values, a deliberate attack on those who wish to promote merit and excellence, a deliberate attack on our heritage and great past. There are those who gnaw away at our national self-respect, re-writing British history as centuries of unrelieved gloom, oppression and failure, as days of hopelessness, not Days of Hope.

Speech to the Conservative Party Conference, 10/10/75

[Britain is] no longer in the politics of the pendulum, but of the ratchet.

Speech to the Institute of Public Relations, 2/11/77

I regard all those who use force to get their own way, who want to destroy our way of life, as Left.

The Times, 29/8/77

Some socialists seem to believe that people should be numbers in a state computer. We believe they should be individuals.

Speech to the Conservative Party Conference, 10/10/75

Q. How would you like your premiership and your government to be regarded in history?

A. I really think that it was the turn of the tide. We were slipping so fast into a socialist state, that the individual mattered less and the collective more. That is not right for the British character.

The Times, 28/3/86

We were elected to do certain things and the real difficulty of this country is that the Labour Party is financed by the trade unions and therefore any advice they give is obviously not without prejudice.

The Times, 5/5/80

————◄◆◆►————

Those people, particularly those in the House, who yelp and yawl at me every day, aren't worried about my policies *failing*. That's not why they want me to change them. They're trying to knock me off those policies because they believe they will *succeed*.

Daily Mail, 3/5/80

[Of Labour attacks in the Commons.] I must say the adrenalin flows when they really come out fighting at me and I fight back and I stand there and I know: 'Now come on, Maggie, you are wholly on your own. No one can help you.' And I love it.

The Times, 1/12/80

The criticism has been vicious, but in the end, you have to build an armour round yourself, knowing the things they say aren't true. I think it's worse for my husband, having to sit back and listen to it all. When he sees me tired, of course he says 'Why don't you give this job up?' My greatest strength, I think, is that come what may, I somehow cope.

Daily Mail, 8/2/72

[On marriage.] It dawned on me that this was the biggest thing in one's life now kind of sorted out and, therefore, one turned one's mind to other things.

The Times, 20/11/85

I had the children the day we won the Ashes – *do* I remember. It was a Saturday and we couldn't find my husband anywhere. The twins took rather a long time to arrive and *he* had mooched off somewhere.

Patricia Murray, *Margaret Thatcher: A Profile*, 1980

There was not a lot of fun and sparkle in my life. I tried to give my children more.

Talk to under-twelves at Grantham High School for Girls, 6/6/80

Parents don't want what is called positive images for gays being forced on innocent children.

Address to the Tory Central Council in Torquay, 21/3/87

You have to tell your children what's right and wrong and you must obviously have some rules, but you don't want rules for the sake of rules and you must explain them. They ask endless questions and you need endless patience but you have got to explain, you've got to try and give them answers. One of the great problems today is that some parents don't talk to their young children enough. Now I was lucky, I had someone in to help with the twins and I was told how important it was to talk to them. When you pick them up and bath them, there should be a continuous round of chatting. Of course mothers are always busy and there are a lot of pressures but you have to try to find time to explain things.

Patricia Murray, *Margaret Thatcher: A Profile,* **1980**

What we are now trying to do is to make certain in the whole of the western world, that we never let our guard down. Never, so long as we keep our guard up, I don't believe we shall get a world war . . . So please recognize that your government must spend enough on defence to see that the third world war never comes about.

Talk to under-twelves at Grantham High School for Girls, 6/6/80

Who would rejoice if Britain came out [of Europe]? The Warsaw Pact countries. They would have their tight alliance and would see that the democracies could not work together in peace. We can and we do. Of course, there will be difficult times – the closer the family is, the more virulent the quarrels.

Time, 16/2/81

[On Trident.] I do not recognize a moral case against it.

The Times, 10/4/84

People who go out prepared to take the lives of other people forfeit their own right to live.

The Times, 16/10/84

I personally have always supported capital punishment. I think that the vast majority of people in this country would like to see the death penalty restored. It isn't that I wish to see it used a very great deal.

The Times, 26/4/79

[Victorian values] were the values when our country became great.

Weekend World, 16/1/82

————◄◆◆►————

When you go abroad now, instead of local people saying to you: 'Oh yes, you British, your country is going down the drain,' they now say: 'Ah Britain, there are a lot of interesting things going on there, aren't there?' They are actually interested in you and your country. They know we are trying a whole new approach, and that Britain can be a world leader again.

Daily Mail, 3/5/80

[On Britain.] The greatest place on earth for a holiday.

The Times, 14/6/86

Wherever I go I am offered Perrier water. I get very irritated. I get it when [we] have a perfectly good British alternative.

Sun, 9/7/85

Other people still believe we can do it [achieve future prosperity]. But, if I give up, we will lose. If I give that up, I just think we will lose all that faith in the future. We'd lose the justification. I hope that doesn't sound too . . . arrogant.

The Sunday Times, 3/8/80

We're going to do it by creating the conditions for real jobs, not artificial ones, so that once again the products stream from our factories and workshops while the customers of the world scramble over each other to buy them.

Pre-election Speech, Birmingham, 19/4/79

The Socialists' battle cry is always the same. 'The Conservatives,' they say, 'want unemployment.' 'Conservative cuts,' they claim, 'would double or treble those out of work.' Now this is nonsense and we must recognize it as nonsense.

The Times, 9/10/76

I think that we will be out of the wood in two or three years.

The Times, 20/3/80

Unemployment should begin to come down by around the middle of my next Parliament.

BBC TV News, Interview, 8/6/83

[Accusing those who complained about the effects of unemployment of being 'moaning minnies'.] Now stop it. You want more jobs and so do I. Now cheer up and go and boost the successes and you are much more likely to get jobs.

Guardian, 12/9/85

People are reluctant to move, even a comparatively small distance, to take new jobs.

This is a natural reaction. What woman welcomes the turmoil of moving house? Who wants to separate herself from old friends and neighbours, to set about finding new schools for the children and discovering by experiment who is the best local butcher? . . . There must be some mobility of labour. If people are not willing to move as their fathers did, the economy cannot thrive.

The Times, 21/7/80

We are tackling the fundamental causes of un-employment ... Quick cures are quack cures. They don't work, they don't last and they won't do.

Daily Mail, 8/6/83

Our policies will produce more jobs in the future.

Speech at a Conservative PPC meeting, 18/5/83

If people would work for the amount of money they are receiving in unemployed pay and social security in the public sector, the extra we would have to find would be the materials, the supervision and the premises. Maybe that would be possible. But to suggest to them that they work for that – I am afraid that they just simply would not. Indeed, as you know, there are a number of jobs for which people will not come forward because they reckon they receive more on social security.

Sunday Telegraph, 14/2/82

Some of our friends were unemployed and what we had we shared with them.

Patricia Murray, *Margaret Thatcher: A Profile*, 1980

As you know, I do not take the full amount [in salary] that I could myself, because one tries to do it by way of example.

Sunday Telegraph, 14/2/82

[To an interviewer in Ottawa.] You, too, have unemployment in the United States . . .

The Times, 27/9/83

What they are saying is absolute poppycock and people
really aren't taking any notice of it. There is absolutely
no comparison between today and the 1930s, none
whatsoever.

The Times, 5/5/80

There is no government definition of poverty . . . There are many . . . definitions of poverty . . . they are wholly artificial definitions. The fact remains that people who are living in need are fully and properly provided for.

Hansard, 22/12/83

We are in touch with real people and the real world.

Speech in Fleetwood, 7/6/83

We have been accused of cuts in services where there have been increases. The only accusation that can justifiably be made is that we do not shout loudly enough about our achievements.

The Times, 23/5/85

The NHS is safe with us.

Conservative Party Conference, 8/10/82

We are not intending ... to dismantle the Welfare State.

The Times, 18/2/83

I have no more intention of dismantling the National Health Service than I have of dismantling Britain's defences.

Speech in Edinburgh, 31/5/83

We must always run our tax system so those who are the great providers of our country find it worthwhile to carry out their creative work. On them success and the future of our welfare services depend. The economic policies I follow are very similar to those in which [Churchill] believed – trying to keep your expenditure within your budget. Why should some people think that revolutionary when it is what every housewife and businessman knows?

Speech in Dumfries, 31/8/83

[During an interview at 10 Downing Street.] You saw the last thing I did in there was to switch every light off? ... And why did I do it? Firstly, I'm on public sector money, and therefore I'm bound to be careful. But also I know that's what every person has to do when they walk out of a room in their own home.

The Sunday Times, 3/8/80

My policies are based not on some economic theory, but on things I and millions like me were brought up with: An honest day's work for an honest day's pay. Live within your means. Put a nest-egg by for a rainy day. Pay your bills on time. Support the police.

News of the World, 20/9/81

It's something of a mystery as to why sterling is falling.

The Times, 17/1/85

I very rarely have an explanation for what happens in the stock market.

The Times, 1/6/84

Politics is the art of finding solutions to problems. But some of the problems wouldn't exist if it weren't for the politicians.

Daily Telegraph, 26/5/69

Where there is discord, may we bring harmony.
Where there is error, may we bring truth.
Where there is doubt, may we bring faith.
Where there is despair, may we bring hope.

Entering Downing Street, May 1979

———◄◄►►———

It is perhaps trite to say so (but most trite things have stood for thousands of years) but freedom would not last unless we have freedom of the press. And freedom of the press would not last unless you have commercial freedom. Never let government interfere with the press, you would lose everything you hold most dear.

The Times, 17/4/80

[On media coverage of the Falklands War.] I understand that there are times when it seems that we and the Argentines are being treated almost as equals and almost on a neutral basis. I understand that there are occasions when some commentators will say that the Argentines did something and then 'the British' did something. I can only say that if this is so it gives offence and causes great emotion among many people.

Robert Harris, *Gotcha!; The Media, the Government and the Falklands Crisis*, 1983

◄◆◆►

The government have explained very fully and on numerous occasions both in this House and in another place the reasons for the attack on the *General Belgrano*. An inquiry into the affair would therefore serve no useful purpose.

Clive Ponting, *The Right to Know: The Inside Story of the Belgrano Affair*, 1985

Everyone agrees that the *Belgrano* had to be sunk. At least I hope they do.

TV AM, 8/6/85

But it was not sailing away from the Falklands.

Clive Ponting, *The Right to Know:*
The Inside Story of the Belgrano Affair, 1985

[Of the *Belgrano* affair.] There has been no attempt whatsoever to mislead the House. No attempt whatsoever.

House of Commons, 14/2/85

I shall continue to give the facts, to be fair, and to be the essence of sweet-reasonableness.

Hansard, 28/7/83

Do you think . . . that I spend my days prowling round the pigeon-holes of the Ministry of Defence to look at the chart of each and every ship? If you do you must be bonkers!

TV AM, 8/6/85

◄◆◆►

[On her premiership.] It is just like having a new suit, the longer you wear it the more it fits you. You sort of feel happier in it. It suits me. What can I say? I think most people grow into a job. Most people gain by coming through baptismal fire and, my goodness, I have been through it. You come out strengthened, really strengthened, and I do not find any difficulty in handling the volume of work at all, none whatever, but then I am a worker. My family were workers – work is our life.

Sunday Telegraph, 14/2/82

If a woman like Eva Peron with no ideals can get that far, think how far I can go with all the ideals that I have.

The Sunday Times, 23/11/80

Just remember this. If you are to be a leader you don't just sit back and mutter sweet nothings or just listen and do nothing. That's not the essence of leadership.

Daily Mail, 3/5/80

I love being at the centre of things.

Reader's Digest, January 1984

Denis does like a bit of glitter.

The Times, 17/11/86

I like to be made a fuss of by a lot of chaps.

Daily Mirror, 14/2/75

[On Marks and Spencer's undergarments.]
Love them! Who doesn't!

The Times, 20/11/86

I used to love wearing black till I turned up at a dinner party in it and found every other woman in it too. It's been colour for me ever since.

Daily Telegraph, 5/10/64

Denis loves bright colours, like this fuchsia dress. But it's really not practical – people remember if they've seen you in pink and think you've only got one outfit.

The Times, 17/11/86

[On clothes.] Movement, that's the thing. I'm always in and out of cars. Can't be jersey, that seats. And it must – don't you agree – be blue?

Daily Telegraph, 5/10/64

I'd always been happiest in fairly high heels, so low ones wouldn't be any help even now. I get them re-heeled every two days. The repairer is wonderfully quick – I think he must be on our side.

Daily Telegraph, 5/10/64

Since shoulders are wider, we have been putting in shoulder pads and lengthening hems. You know, you should never press a hem like a knife edge, or you'll never be able to let it down again.

The Times, 17/11/86

[On campaign comfort.] I always feel most at ease in a suit; an inexpensive Chanel copy suits me perfectly. The matching blouse is important, as one encounters so many temperatures during a campaign day.

Daily Telegraph, 5/10/64

The only poll I am interested in is the poll which is taken on general election day.

The Times, 21/2/85

I am certain that we will win the general election with a good majority. Not that I am ever over-confident.

London Evening Standard, 17/3/87

——◄◆◆►——

Conservatives are, and always have been, British nationalists, stressing the word 'British'.

Speech in Glasgow, 21/2/75

[UK passports] are not looked on as just British but *Oh! British!* Interesting . . .

The Times, 22/5/80

Unless we change our ways and our direction, our greatness as a nation will soon be a footnote in the history books, a distant memory of an off-shore island lost in the mists of time, like Camelot, remembered kindly for its noble past.

The Times, 2/5/79

It is not as if we have great wide open spaces or great natural resources, we have not. So, either you go on taking in 40 or 50,000 a year, which is far too many, or you say we must hold out the prospect of a clear end to immigration and that is the view we have taken and I am certain that is the right view to keep good race relations and to keep fundamental British characteristics which have done so much for the world.

World in Action, 30/1/78

We want to know how many dependants have the right [to join their immigrant parents]. If it were 500,000, we just could not take them.

We have to find out how many under the present law are entitled to settle here. If the enquiries indicate that a very large number are entitled to come, we should have to change the law or take them in under a very small quota each year.

The Times, 5/10/76

At the moment it is about between 45,000 and 50,000 people coming in a year. Now, I was brought up in a small town, 25,000. That would be two new towns a year and that is quite a lot. So, we do have to hold out the prospect of an end to immigration except, of course, for compassionate cases.

World in Action, 30/1/78

I heard on the radio yesterday that staffing in hotels is frequently from people who are neither British immigrants nor from the EEC. They're still coming in. This is ridiculous. I'll tell you why: . . . *our* youngsters should be getting those jobs.

The Sunday Times, 3/8/80

When I went round India and Pakistan . . . I said to them: 'You do realize that this country, the United Kingdom, is more densely populated than either India or Pakistan.'

World in Action, 30/1/78

Well now, we did make a very considerable cutback, as you remember, in 1971. We said after that – and the Act took effect in 1973 – everyone coming in no longer had the right to settle permanently in this country. Now that was quite a major step forward.

World in Action, 30/1/78

There is no racism in the Conservative Party. We believe in equal opportunities for all our citizens, whatever their background.

Hansard, 2/2/84

◆◆◆◆

I shall not make it a major election issue but I think there is a feeling that the big political parties have not been talking about this and sometimes, you know, we are falsely accused of racial prejudice. I say 'Falsely accused' and that means we do not talk about it perhaps as much as we should. In my view, that is one thing that is driving some people to the National Front. They do not agree with the objectives of the National Front, but they say that at least they are talking about some of the problems.

World in Action, 30/1/78

Q. So some of the support that the National Front has been attracting in recent by-elections you would hope to bring back behind the Tory Party?

A. Oh, very much so, certainly. But I think that the National Front has, in fact, attracted more people from Labour voters than from us; but never be afraid to tackle something which people are worried about. We are not in politics to ignore people's worries: we are in politics to deal with them.

World in Action, 30/1/78

We have no extremes in our party. We have four years' record behind us. There has been nothing extreme and there is nothing extreme in this manifesto.

The Times, 7/6/83

We have been trying to teach the relevance of what is taught. Last September, we launched a new scheme that will give fourteen- to eighteen-year-olds the chance to take a four-year technical or vocational course directly related to the needs of firms in their area. Once they can see the point of learning, their whole attitude changes.

Reader's Digest, January 1984

[Children] ought to know a little about commerce and industry, and what is expected of them in commerce and industry ... Unfortunately, in our education system youngsters are still not given sufficient encouragement to go into industry or commerce, and not told that is a good thing to make an honest profit. They should be told that if you don't make a profit, you won't be in business for very long because you haven't anything to plough back for tomorrow. And you make your profit by pleasing others. So you have to make it honestly.

Director, September 1983

[Comprehensives] have often been working best in Tory areas and for a very simple reason. It is not only because these are more homogeneous areas but because their parents are passionately concerned about their children's education.

The Sunday Times, 15/11/70

People from my sort of background need good schools to compete with children from privileged homes like Shirley Williams and Anthony Wedgwood Benn.

The Sunday Times, 16/10/77

I see no fundamental difficulty in selling milk in schools. I myself bought it as a primary school pupil many years ago, and it was not too difficult then.

Hansard, 18/11/71

Although you can learn a lot from television, you must do things yourselves. You must be doers and not watchers.

Talk to under-twelves at Grantham High School for Girls, 6/6/80

Sometimes I think I have heard enough about restraint. It was not restraint that brought us the achievements of Elizabethan England or started the Industrial Revolution. It was not restraint that led Lord Nuffield to start building cars in a bicycle shop in Oxford.

It was not restraint that inspired us to explore for oil in the North Sea and bring it ashore. It was incentive. Positive, vital, driving incentive. The incentive that was once the dynamo of this country but which our youth today are denied. Incentive that has been snuffed out by the Socialist State.

The Times, 9/10/76

When you take into public ownership a profitable industry, the profits soon disappear. The goose that laid the golden eggs goes broody. State geese are not great layers.

Speech to Finchley Constituents, 31/1/76

There are too few rich and too few profits ... The unprofitability of an employer, caused by wage and salary increases that outrun improvements in productivity in sales, is a very clear and unambiguous signal to the work force.

Speech to the Conservative National Union Executive, 13/6/75

Yes, I can give you examples of companies where employees have struck themselves out of jobs. And I say to them, don't blame your unemployment on me. It is your fault.

The Sunday Times, 5/5/81

At a time of unemployment, the government has deliberately created 60,000 more unemployed. That is not my way.

The Times, 5/10/76

How has he managed to achieve the disastrous double of 1,500,000 people out of work and shortage of skilled labour? ... He will go down in history as the Prime Minister for Unemployment.

The Times, 25/1/78

◄◆◆►

Let Labour's Orwellian nightmare of the left be the spur for us to dedicate with a new urgency our every ounce of moral strength to rebuild the fortunes of this free nation. If we were to fail, that freedom could be imperilled. So let us resist the blandishments of the faint-hearts; let us ignore the howls and threats of the extremists, let us stand together, and do our duty, and we shall not fail.

Speech to the Conservative Party Conference, 10/10/80

Communism is the left foot of socialism, and Fascism the right foot, using socialism in the sense that it is total regimentation and control by the state.

The Times, 29/8/77

[To Labour demonstrators.] You stand there shouting because you have no arguments. How pathetic the party you support. How pathetic you are. Just standing there shouting and with banners because you have not got any arguments left.

The Times, 9/6/83

I think some people are absolutely fed up to the back teeth at some of these protesters, the way they do their protesting and the mess they leave: the terrible mess they leave, and the amount of time they require from the police.

The Times, 31/3/83

————◄◆◆►————

Why not 'Maggie'? It's rather homely and I quite like it. Anyway, it's shorter for newspaper headlines. You've such a job making 'Margaret' fit ... I always appreciate the other person's problem.

Daily Express, 13/8/80

———◄◄◆►———

[On the Toxteth riots in July 1981.] Oh, those poor shopkeepers.

Ed. Hugo Young and Anne Sloman,
The Thatcher Phenomenon, 1981

I am only too delighted to do everything we can to make life difficult for such things as hippie convoys.

House of Commons, 5/6/86

I was brought up very, very seriously. I was a very serious child and we were not allowed to go out to much entertainment. Going out to a film was a very great treat.

Talk to under-twelves at Grantham High School for Girls, 6/6/80

I don't think I ever went to a dance until I went to university. Dancing was frowned upon by my parents – dancing was forbidden. I was allowed to learn ballet and eurhythmics because that was cultural, but everything always had to have some cultural content.

Patricia Murray, *Margaret Thatcher: A Profile*, 1980

I went to church four times on a Sunday and I owe a great deal to the Church for everything in which I believe. I am very glad that I was brought up strictly.

Talk to under-twelves at Grantham High School for Girls, 6/6/80

[On James Anderton's divinely-inspired remarks regarding AIDS.] I am very glad that some people have spoken out . . . Some people have made their position very clear – thank goodness for that.

The Times, 24/1/87

I think I was probably closer to my father but my mother was a good woman who was always intensely practical and I learned a lot of practical stuff from her. She taught me how to cook and bake bread, how to make my own clothes and how to decorate. We always used to decorate our own home because we could never afford to have decorators in and I've always liked doing things with my hands.

Patricia Murray, *Margaret Thatcher: A Profile*, 1980

The warmth of your family and keeping that relationship bright and alive will mean more to you than anything else.

Getting Married (EMJ booklet), 1985

I loved my mother dearly but after I was fifteen we had nothing more to say to each other. It wasn't her fault. She was weighed down by the home, always being in the home.

Daily Telegraph, 5/2/75

—◄◆◆►—

I cry. What human being with any sensitivity wouldn't? Men cry too. There's nothing wrong with crying at the appropriate time.

Daily Mail, 10/9/79

Well, there are two sides of me, the informal friendly me and the iron touch, the Iron Lady. But just because you have to demonstrate iron from time to time, that doesn't mean that it should show through the whole time.

Daily Mail, 3/5/80

If you saw me writing a speech at four o'clock in the morning, with my make-up gone and running my hands through my hair, you'd get a different picture.

Daily Express, 13/8/80

◄◆◆►

[On what she likes to do at the weekends.] Popping up to the little flat at the top of Number Ten and doing a poached egg on toast.

Talk to under-twelves at Grantham High School for Girls, 6/6/80

I still tidy round myself at weekends, but I'm afraid I don't do much dusting. And my cooking – I used to be good – is the simple stuff now. Shepherd's pie, or fling in an omelette or a casserole – nothing complicated.

Daily Express, 13/8/80

My pleasure reading ... is the John le Carré kind of thing, which I love; of course, I do read biography, and some philosophy and anything in connection with the home. I love going through the *House and Garden* magazines, seeing what these people are doing who have time and money to do it.

The Times, 5/5/80

[On shopping.] I catch sight of something in a window and rush straight back for it.

Daily Telegraph, 5/10/64

You mustn't win on everything the whole time. So you fight on the thing that really matters and you let the others go. I've got to get this, you think. But the other doesn't matter so much, there is another view and you accept it. You just know these things, it's a combination of intuition and experience. Most of life is a combination of these two things.

Daily Mail, 3/5/80

People can be so vicious, and if you pay too much attention you get a complex about yourself. People always try to topple you, but they won't win. I read very, very little about myself. If there's a snide remark I know it could put me off for two or three hours, maybe stop me concentrating, so I don't look.

Daily Express, 13/8/80

I have no idea why people keep attacking me. I don't think I deserve it at all.

Sunday Express, 16/1/72

I think children are afraid of the dark . . . There's no point in trying to make them get used to the dark, most children are afraid of the dark and it's much easier for them to have a very dim light so that they can just wake up and see that everything is all right.

Patricia Murray, *Margaret Thatcher: A Profile*, 1980

FOR THE BEST IN PAPERBACKS, LOOK FOR THE

A CHOICE OF PENGUINS AND PELICANS

The Second World War (6 volumes)   Winston S. Churchill

The definitive history of the cataclysm which swept the world for the second time in thirty years.

1917: The Russian Revolutions and the Origins of Present-Day Communism
Leonard Schapiro

A superb narrative history of one of the greatest episodes in modern history by one of our greatest historians.

Imperial Spain 1496–1716   J. H. Elliot

A brilliant modern study of the sudden rise of a barren and isolated country to be the greatest power on earth, and of its equally sudden decline. 'Outstandingly good' – *Daily Telegraph*

Joan of Arc: The Image of Female Heroism   Marina Warner

'A profound book, about human history in general and the place of women in it' – Christopher Hill

FOR THE BEST IN PAPERBACKS, LOOK FOR THE

A CHOICE OF PENGUINS AND PELICANS

The Apartheid Handbook Roger Omond

This book provides the essential hard information about how apartheid actually works from day to day and fills in the details behind the headlines.

The World Turned Upside Down Christopher Hill

This classic study of radical ideas during the English Revolution 'will stand as a notable monument to . . . one of the finest historians of the present age' – *The Times Literary Supplement*

Islam in the World Malise Ruthven

'His exposition of "the Qurenic world view" is the most convincing, and the most appealing, that I have read' – Edward Mortimer in *The Times*

The Knight, the Lady and the Priest Georges Duby

'A very fine book' (Philippe Aries) that traces back to its medieval origin one of our most important institutions, modern marriage.

A Social History of England New Edition Asa Briggs

'A treasure house of scholarly knowledge . . . beautifully written and full of the author's love of his country, its people and its landscape' – John Keegan in the *Sunday Times*, Books of the Year

A CHOICE OF PENGUINS AND PELICANS

The French Revolution   Christopher Hibbert

'One of the best accounts of the Revolution that I know . . . Mr Hibbert is outstanding' – J. H. Plumb in the *Sunday Telegraph*

The Germans   Gordon A. Craig

An intimate study of a complex and fascinating nation by 'one of the ablest and most distinguished American historians of modern Germany' – Hugh Trevor-Roper

Ireland: A Positive Proposal   Kevin Boyle and Tom Hadden

A timely and realistic book on Northern Ireland which explains the historical context – and offers a practical and coherent set of proposals which could actually work.

A History of Venice   John Julius Norwich

'Lord Norwich has loved and understood Venice as well as any other Englishman has ever done' – Peter Levi in the *Sunday Times*

A CHOICE OF PENGUINS

Castaway Lucy Irvine

'Writer seeks "wife" for a year on a tropical island.' This is the extraordinary, candid, sometimes shocking account of what happened when Lucy Irvine answered the advertisement, and found herself embroiled in what was not exactly a desert island dream. 'Fascinating' – *Daily Mail*

Out of Africa Karen Blixen (Isak Dinesen)

After the failure of her coffee-farm in Kenya, where she lived from 1913 to 1931, Karen Blixen went home to Denmark and wrote this unforgettable account of her experiences. 'No reader can put the book down without some share in the author's poignant farewell to her farm' – *Observer*

The Lisle Letters Edited by Muriel St Clare Byrne

An intimate, immediate and wholly fascinating picture of a family in the reign of Henry VIII. 'Remarkable . . . we can really hear the people of early Tudor England talking' – Keith Thomas in the *Sunday Times*. 'One of the most extraordinary works to be published this century' – J. H. Plumb

A CHOICE OF PENGUINS

Adieux: A Farewell to Sartre   Simone de Beauvoir

A devastatingly frank account of the last years of Sartre's life, and his death, by the woman who for more than half a century shared that life. 'A true labour of love, there is about it a touching sadness, a mingling of the personal with the impersonal and timeless which Sartre himself would surely have liked and understood' – *Listener*

Business Wargames   James Barrie

How did BMW overtake Mercedes? Why did Laker crash? How did McDonalds grab the hamburger market? Drawing on the tragic mistakes and brilliant victories of military history, this remarkable book draws countless fascinating parallels with case histories from industry world-wide.

Metamagical Themas   Douglas R. Hofstadter

This astonishing sequel to the best-selling, Pulitzer Prize-winning *Gödel, Escher, Bach* swarms with 'extraordinary ideas, brilliant fables, deep philosophical questions and Carrollian word play' – Martin Gardner

FOR THE BEST IN PAPERBACKS, LOOK FOR THE

A CHOICE OF PENGUINS

An African Winter Preston King With an Introduction by Richard Leakey

This powerful and impassioned book offers a unique assessment of the interlocking factors which result in the famines of Africa and argues that there *are* solutions and we *can* learn from the mistakes of the past.

Jean Rhys: Letters 1931–66
Edited by Francis Wyndham and Diana Melly

'Eloquent and invaluable . . . her life emerges, and with it a portrait of an unexpectedly indomitable figure' – Marina Warner in the *Sunday Times*

Among the Russians Colin Thubron

One man's solitary journey by car across Russia provides an enthralling and revealing account of the habits and idiosyncrasies of a fascinating people. 'He sees things with the freshness of an innocent and the erudition of a scholar' – *Daily Telegraph*

The Amateur Naturalist Gerald Durrell with Lee Durrell

'Delight . . . on every page . . . packed with authoritative writing, learning without pomposity . . . it represents a real bargain' – *The Times Educational Supplement*. 'What treats are in store for the average British household' – *Books and Bookmen*

A CHOICE OF PENGUINS

The Book Quiz Book Joseph Connolly

Who was literature's performing flea . . .? Who wrote 'Live Now, Pay Later . . .'? Keats and Cartland, Balzac and Braine, Coleridge conundrums, Eliot enigmas, Tolstoy teasers . . . all in this brilliant quiz book. You will be on the shelf without it . . .

Voyage through the Antarctic Richard Adams and Ronald Lockley

Here is the true, authentic Antarctic of today, brought vividly to life by Richard Adams, author of *Watership Down*, and Ronald Lockley, the world-famous naturalist. 'A good adventure story, with a lot of information and a deal of enthusiasm for Antarctica and its animals' – *Nature*

Getting to Know the General Graham Greene

'In August 1981 my bag was packed for my fifth visit to Panama when the news came to me over the telephone of the death of General Omar Torrijos Herrera, my friend and host . . .' 'Vigorous, deeply felt, at times funny, and for Greene surprisingly frank' – *Sunday Times*